John Thompson's Easiest Piano Course

PART SIX

Copyright, MCMLVI, by The Willis Music Co.
International Copyright Secured
Printed in U. S. A.

7777 W. BLUEMOUND RD. P.O. BOX 13819 MILWAUKEE, WI 53213

Contents

	Page
FOREWORD	3
ALLA BREVE	
"The Midget Racer"	4
"Boogie Woogie"	6
FROM THE CLASSICS	
"Grandmother's Minuet" (arr.) . . Grieg	8
TRIPLETS	
"Etude in Triplets"	10
TRIPLETS IN TWO-FOUR	
"The Ranger"	11
TRIPLETS IN THREE-FOUR	
"On the Village Green"	12
TRIPLETS IN FOUR-FOUR	
"Habanera" from the Opera, Carmen (arr.) Bizet	14
HARPSICHORD STYLE	
"Sonatina"	16
AN OLD FAVORITE	
"Flower Song" (arr.) . . . . . Lange	18
WRIST STACCATO	
"When Johnny Comes Marching Home" (arr.) . . . . Gilmore	20
THE DOTTED EIGHTH NOTE	21
THE DOTTED EIGHTH IN THREE-FOUR	
"Minuet" from Septet (arr.) . . Beethoven	22
THE DOTTED EIGHTH IN FOUR-FOUR	
"The School Band"	24
MELODY IN INNER VOICE	
"The Lily Pond"	26
THE TRILL	
"Bird Song"	28
SYNCOPATION	
"Jam Session"	30
FROM THE CLASSICS	
"Liebestraum No. 3" (arr.) . . . . Liszt	32
CROSS HAND	
"The Fountain"	34
CHORD STUDY	
"Evening Harmonies"	36
DESCRIPTIVE PIECE	
"Hobgoblins"	39
STUDY IN STYLE	
"Gypsy Life"	42
MARCH	
"Semper Fidelis" (arr.) . . . . . Sousa	44
FORMING MINOR SCALES	47
CERTIFICATE	48

Foreword

PART SIX introduces Alla Breve, the Triplet, Dotted Eighth Notes, Melody lying in the inner voices, the Trill, Syncopation and several pianistic figures which should be learned as a standard part of every player's technic because of their frequent recurrence in piano music.

The examples offer ample opportunity for review of both technical and musical points learned earlier in the Course and are designed to develop artistry and musicianship to a higher degree of attainment. Pieces calling for the use of Finger Legato, Wrist Staccato, Phrasing, Forearm Attack in Chord Playing, Scale Figures, Pedal, etc., will be found in logical order.

SUPPLEMENTARY MATERIAL

Since it is impossible to put into one book material to meet the needs of all its various users, it is expected that the teacher will assign whatever supplementary material is indicated by the individual pupil. This is particularly true in matters technical, where students show a wide variance.

The following books are suggested as being especially fitted for use as supplementary work for pupils in this grade.

John Thompson's SCALE SPELLER — A Writing Book for Home Work which teaches Major and Minor Scales in all forms. Also teaches Intervals.

John Thompson's FIFTY SECOND GRADE ETUDES — Etudes from Bertini, Czerny, Duvernoy, Heller, etc., carefully selected and adapted for use in Second Grade.

John Thompson's TUNEFUL TECHNIC — Technical figures from recognized masters of etude-writing have been taken and woven into or around well-known tunes — thus giving the pupil the benefit of the original exercise PLUS the pleasure of playing favorite airs.

John Thompson

Alla Breve

You have already learned that this sign (**C**) means four-four. That is, there will be four counts to each measure and one count to each quarter note.

But when you see the same sign used with a line through it like this (**₵**), it is called *alla breve* and means there will be only TWO counts to the measure and one count to each HALF NOTE.

The alla breve sign does not change the rhythmical divisions in the least. It simply means the piece will be played twice as fast as though it were written in Four-Four and thus it would be uncomfortable to count or beat four times per measure. By cutting the counting in half (one count to each half note) it makes the piece sound as though it were written in Two-Four.

You will encounter many examples with the alla breve sign. When you do, learn them first in ordinary four-four, then as speed develops, you can begin counting two to each measure — the first count falling on ONE and the second count on what would ordinarily be THREE, the third count.

The Midget Racer

Copyright, MCMLVI, by The Willis Music Co.
International Copyright Secured
Printed in U.S.A.

The following is a characteristic figure used often in BOOGIE WOOGIE. It cannot be called very musical but for some strange reason, many people seem to like it.

It is well to have a few such examples in your repertoire so that when you go to a party and are asked to play, you need not sit back in a corner just because your pieces for the most part are looked upon by some as being the "long-haired" type.

When learning it, practice it just as carefully as if it were a more conventional type of composition. You will at least get some excellent practice in passing over the left hand while the right hand plays chords both in "block" and broken form.

Boogie Woogie

Play this Minuet with light, staccato touch — being sure however to give plenty of resonance to the chords marked with the *sostenuto* sign, i.e., the little black line drawn over or under the chord. Be careful, too, to apply accents as marked. Keep the tempo rather strict throughout.

Edvard Grieg was born in Bergen, Norway in 1843. After studying in Germany, he returned to Norway and devoted himself to the cause of National Norwegian music. At his death in 1916, fifty-seven governments sent official representatives to attend his funeral.

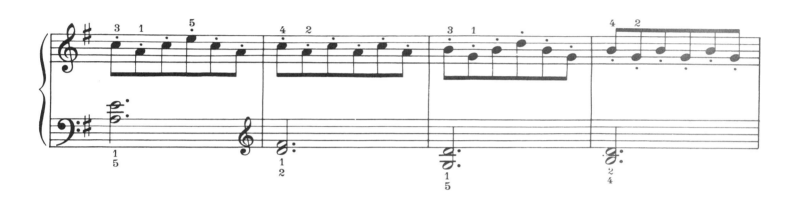

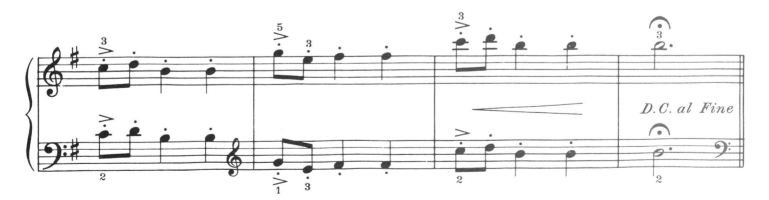

Triplets

TRIPLET is the name given to a group of THREE notes that are intended to be played in the time ordinarily given to TWO notes of equal value.

For instance: — THREE eighth notes played in the time of TWO eighth notes,

OR

THREE quarter notes played in the time of TWO quarter notes and so on.

A figure in ordinary eighths

Similiar figure arranged in triplets

Etude in Triplets

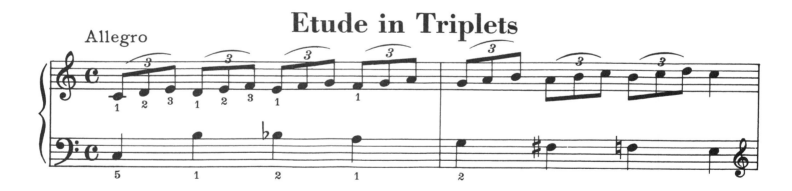

Triplets in Two-Four

The Ranger

Triplets in Three-Four

The following piece employs a Triplet figure which requires the passing under of the Thumb to make a connection with the rest of the Phrase.

This is a finger pattern often encountered in piano music and it should be learned and stored away along with scales, arpeggios and other figures that go into the making of a technical equipment.

On the Village Green

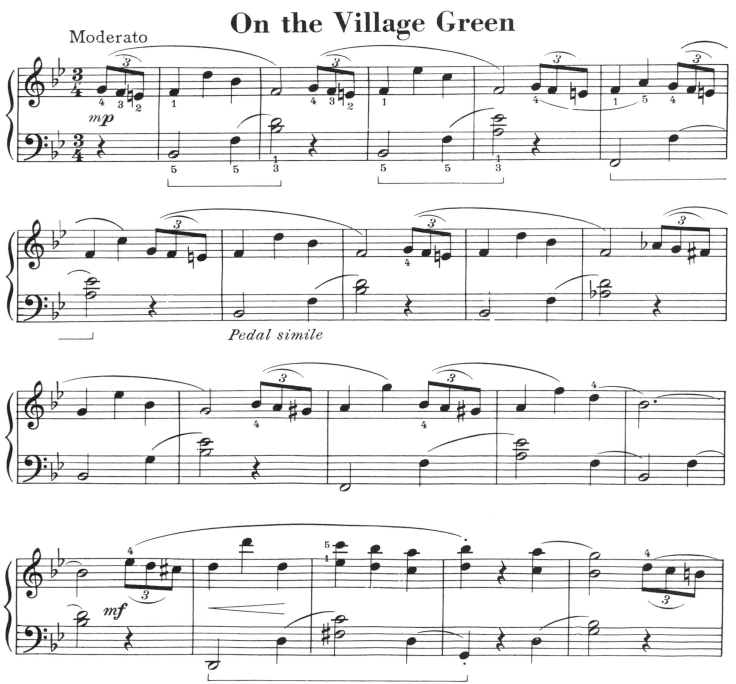

Triplets in Four-Four

The following is an excerpt from the Opera "CARMEN," written by Georges Bizet, a French composer born in Paris, October 25, 1838.

Habanera is a Spanish dance which really dates back to Africa. It was first imported into Cuba by negro slaves, was later modified somewhat and found its way into Spain.

In this piece you will find several examples of a Triplet followed by two eighths. To perform this correctly, simply play three notes (evenly spaced) on the first count, and two notes (evenly spaced) on the second count.

Habanera
from the Opera "CARMEN"

Georges Bizet
(arr.)

Handel at the Harpsichord—Permission of Steinway & Sons

In earlier days, the forerunners of the piano were the Harpsichord, the Clavichord and the Spinet.

These instruments had a tinkling sound compared with the piano of to-day and because they had very little sustaining power, the music written for them contained many graceful ornaments and running passages such as scale and arpeggio figures.

The following is an example of the type of music heard on these instruments. Because of their construction it was necessary to play each key with a sharp, decisive finger attack. When playing this piece, use your best possible finger action and try to imitate the effect of a Harpsichord.

Sonatina

Here is an old tune that was a favorite in your great-grandmother's day.

It was heard as background music in the melodramas of that period and later it was put to the same use in silent movies.

Use the pedal carefully and play the melody with your best possible singing tone.

from
Flower Song

Gustave Lange
(arr.)

Wrist Staccato

This song was composed by Patrick Gilmore during the War between the States. He was, at the time, on duty in New Orleans as bandmaster in General Butler's command. It became very popular among the soldiers who made up many verses of their own to sing while on the march.

Apply a bouncing wrist staccato in the left hand for the first eight measures. Later the accompaniment appears as a broken chord figure which should be rolled, and tossed off sharply.

When Johnny Comes Marching Home

Patrick Gilmore
(arr.)

Allegro con brio

The Dotted Eighth Note

The Dotted Eighth Note is treated exactly the same as other dotted notes you have learned. That is, the dot increases the length of the note by half its value.

Always think of the dot as an imaginary Tie which joins the original note to another note of the same pitch but *next smaller in size*.

Example

Written
The Dotted Half

The dot ties the half note to the next smaller note which is a quarter note.

Played

The Dotted Quarter

The dot ties the quarter note to the next smaller note which is an eighth note.

The Dotted Eighth

The dot ties the eighth note to the next smaller note which is a sixteenth note.

Play the following and notice that the Rhythmical Pattern remains exactly the same whether playing dotted halves, dotted quarters or dotted eighth notes.

All that is changed is the speed (Tempo), each example being twice as fast as the one preceding.

Written

Played

The Dotted Eighth in Three-Four

Beethoven From a painting by Schloesser

The following excerpt from Ludwig van Beethoven is a fine example of the dotted eighth note followed by a sixteenth.

Beethoven must have been very fond of this theme as he made use of it twice — once in a Sonatina for piano and later in his famous Septet for Violin, Viola, 'Cello, Bass, Clarinet, Bassoon and French Horn. The version shown here is the one used in the Septet.

Minuet
from "Septet"

Ludwig van Beethoven
(arr.)

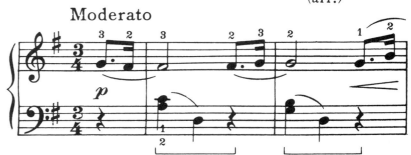

23

The Dotted Eighth in Four-Four

Another example containing dotted eighths. Apply sharp rhythm and keep strict tempo.

The School Band

Melody in Inner Voice

The melody does not always appear in the upper voice. Sometimes it may be in the bass and sometimes in one of the inner voices — alto or tenor.

In the following piece, it will be found in the lower voice of the right hand. Be sure to give it proper significance by making it sing out like a solo part.

The Lily Pond

The Trill

The following piece contains many little trill figures which, when properly played, will imitate bird calls.

Three sets of fingering are given and all three should be learned — one at a time.

After the piece has been thoroughly mastered, try playing it one octave higher than written and you will find the bird effect even more pronounced.

Bird Song

Syncopation

Another example in syncopation.

Be sure to observe all accents and staccato marks as they have a decided bearing on the rhythm.

Jam Session

Franz Liszt, Hungarian musician, was considered one of the greatest pianists of all time. He is probably best remembered for his Hungarian Rhapsodies and the famous *Liebestraum*. He composed three *Liebesträume*, but No. 3 is easily the most popular. The excerpt below is the first theme from the third *Liebestraum* which still enjoys world-wide popularity.

Liebestraum No. 3

Franz Liszt
(arr.)

Cross Hand

Here is a cross-hand piece in which you should try to pass the figures from one hand to the other without any noticeable break.

Play the left hand accompaniment chords with thin staccato so as not to obtrude on the melody tones in the right hand.

The Fountain

Chord Study
Preparatory Exercise

Evening Harmonies

Try to make this piece sound as spooky as possible. Learn it slowly at first, then work up the speed to a very brisk tempo.

Hobgoblins

Allegro vivace

Gypsy music has all the absence of restraint which characterizes this wandering race of people. It is usually in the form of an *Improvisation,* which is to say, it is made up as they go, and therefore follows no set musical pattern. It may start in one Key and end in another and it always follows the varying moods of the performer, ranging from deepest melancholy to fiery abandon.

Usually it begins with a *Lassan* or Lament, which is a slow, mournful song of depression. This breaks, without warning, into a fast and furious dance rhythm, accompanied by the beating of pots and pans by those members of the tribe who lacked musical instruments.

See if you can discover the moods in the following piece and give to it as much contrast as possible.

Gypsy Life

Semper Fidelis
March

John Philip Sousa
(arr.)

Forming Minor Scales
The Parallel Minor Approach

The Parallel Minor scale begins on the same key as the Major scale and is formed by *lowering the 3rd and 6th degrees one half-step.*

The Relative Minor Approach

The Relative Minor scale begins on the 6th degree of the Major scale. It is formed by *raising the 7th degree (of the minor scale) one half-step.*

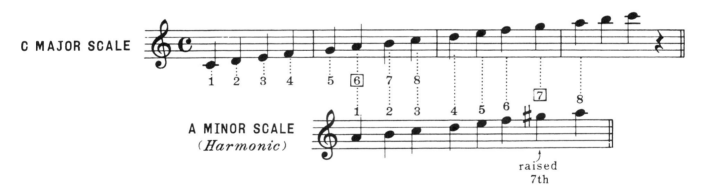

The Parallel Minor scale has the *same Key note* as its Major.

The Relative Minor scale has the *same Key signature* as its Major.

SCALE SPELLER

The examples shown above are for Harmonic Minors only. For practice in Writing, Playing and Analyzing Major and Minor scales in *all forms,* pupils should be assigned John Thompson's SCALE SPELLER, a Writing Book for Home Work. Published by The Willis Music Company.

Certificate of Merit

This certifies that

....

has successfully completed

PART SIX
OF
John Thompson's
EASIEST PIANO COURSE

and is eligible for promotion to

PART SEVEN

....
Teacher

Date ....